T0387658

EVERGLADES

National Park

BY CHRISTINA LEAF

BLASTOFF! DISCOVERY

BELLWETHER MEDIA • MINNEAPOLIS, MN

Blastoff! Discovery launches a new mission: reading to learn. Filled with facts and features, each book offers you an exciting new world to explore!

BLASTOFF! UNIVERSE

GRADE K

GRADES 1-3

GRADE 4

This edition first published in 2024 by Bellwether Media, Inc.

No part of this publication may be reproduced in whole or in part without written permission of the publisher.
For information regarding permission, write to Bellwether Media, Inc.,
Attention: Permissions Department,
6012 Blue Circle Drive, Minnetonka, MN 55343.

Library of Congress Cataloging-in-Publication Data

Names: Leaf, Christina, author.
Title: Everglades National Park / by Christina Leaf.
Description: Minneapolis, MN : Bellwether Media, Inc., 2024. | Series: Blastoff! Discovery : U.S. national parks | Includes bibliographical references and index. | Audience: Ages 7-13 | Audience: Grades 4-6 | Summary: "Engaging images accompany information about Everglades National Park. The combination of high-interest subject matter and narrative text is intended for students in grades 3 through 8"–Provided by publisher.
Identifiers: LCCN 2023045219 (print) | LCCN 2023045220 (ebook) | ISBN 9798886878127 (library binding) | ISBN 9798886879063 (ebook)
Subjects: LCSH: Everglades National Park (Fla.)–Juvenile literature.
Classification: LCC F317.E9 L44 2024 (print) | LCC F317.E9 (ebook) | DDC 975.9/39–dc23/eng/20231002
LC record available at https://lccn.loc.gov/2023045219
LC ebook record available at https://lccn.loc.gov/2023045220

Editor: Rebecca Sabelko
Series Design: Jeffrey Kollock   Book Designer: Laura Sowers

Printed in the United States of America, North Mankato, MN.

TABLE OF CONTENTS

IN THE AIRBOAT

SAWGRASS PRAIRIE

A family is ready to explore Everglades National Park! They climb aboard a wide, flat airboat. A giant fan noisily starts up at the back of the boat. The family passes through tangled **mangroves** as they head into the park.

BIRD WORLD

Everglades National Park is home to more than 360 species of birds!

Soon, they zip past tall stands of sawgrass. The **prairie** stretches as far as the eye can see. Alligators lurk between lily pads in the shallow water. A green heron snaps up a fish. In the distance, a great egret takes flight. There is a wild, wonderful world to see in Everglades National Park!

EVERGLADES NATIONAL PARK

Everglades National Park is part of the famous Everglades **wetland**. The park covers 2,188 square miles (5,667 square kilometers) of southwestern Florida. The city of Miami is to the east. Florida Bay makes up part of the southern areas of the park. The **Gulf** of Mexico lines the park's western edge. Big Cypress National **Preserve** lies just north of the park.

Everglades is famous for its rich **biodiversity**. Many of the species found in the park are not found anywhere else in the world! The park is also known for the threats it faces. People are working hard to protect it.

FLORIDA

N
W + E
S

GULF OF
MEXICO

MIAMI •

FLORIDA
BAY

◼ = EVERGLADES NATIONAL PARK
◼ = BIG CYPRESS NATIONAL PRESERVE

FLORIDA BAY

A BIG PARK

Everglades is the largest national park east of the Mississippi River.

CYPRESS TREES

THE LAND

SAWGRASS PRAIRIE

The area that is now the Everglades was seafloor for millions of years. Limestone built up from shells over time. Around 5,000 years ago, floodwaters from the last **ice age** covered the area. This created the Everglades wetland.

The limestone slopes slightly downward toward the sea. Long ago, the Kissimmee River and Lake Okeechobee would overflow during rainy seasons. The extra water slowly flowed over the land to the Gulf of Mexico. This created a wide, shallow river. Today, much of the river flows through a sawgrass prairie. It creates a "river of grass."

WATER FLOW IN THE EVERGLADES

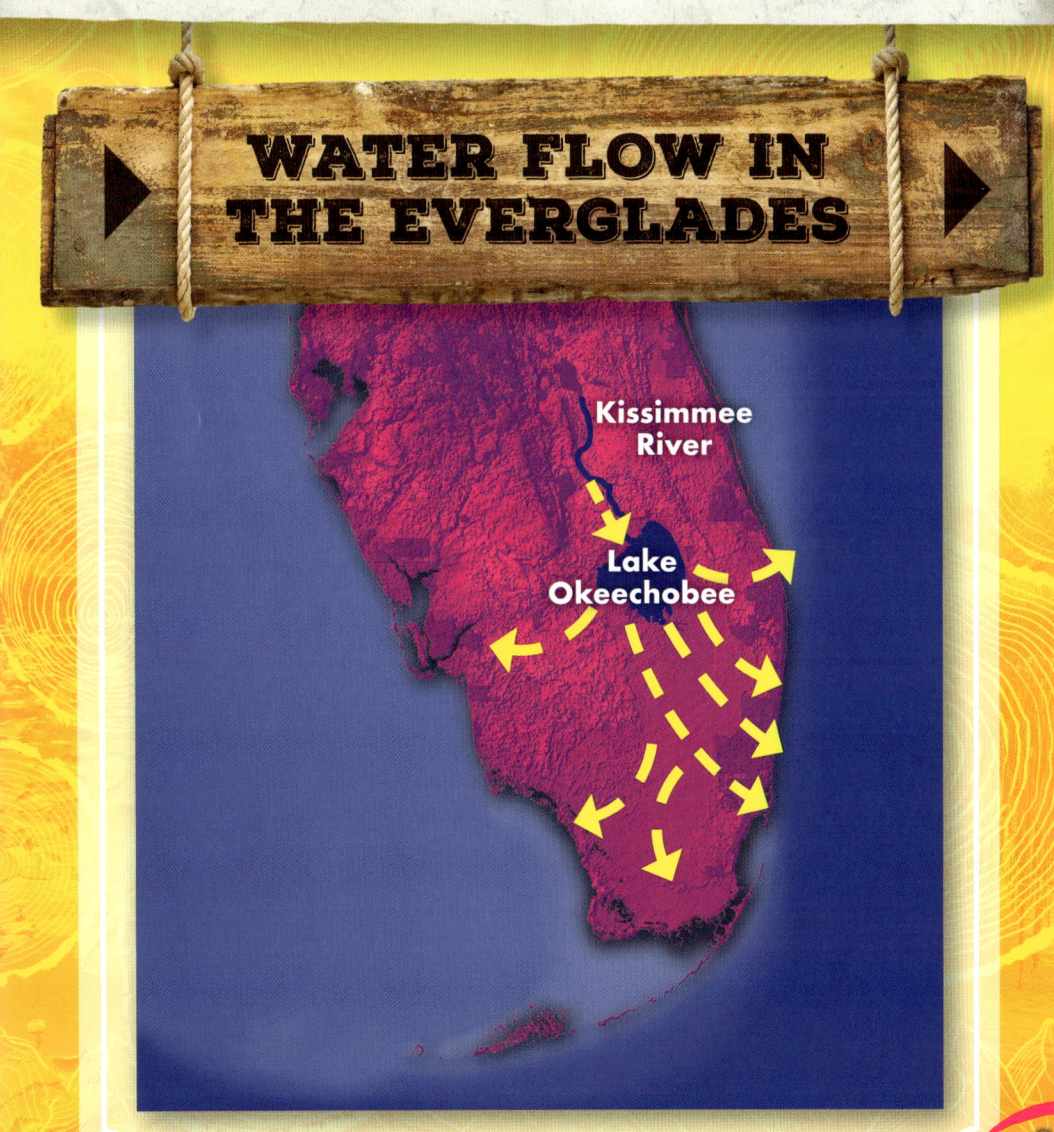

Kissimmee River

Lake Okeechobee

Everglades has many different **habitats**. The highest **elevations** have hardwood trees. Pine rocklands lie below them. Sawgrass prairies cover a large area. The slough is the main waterway through the prairie. Tall cypress trees shade low cypress swamps. Mangrove forests line the coasts. The park also includes Florida Bay and many **estuaries**.

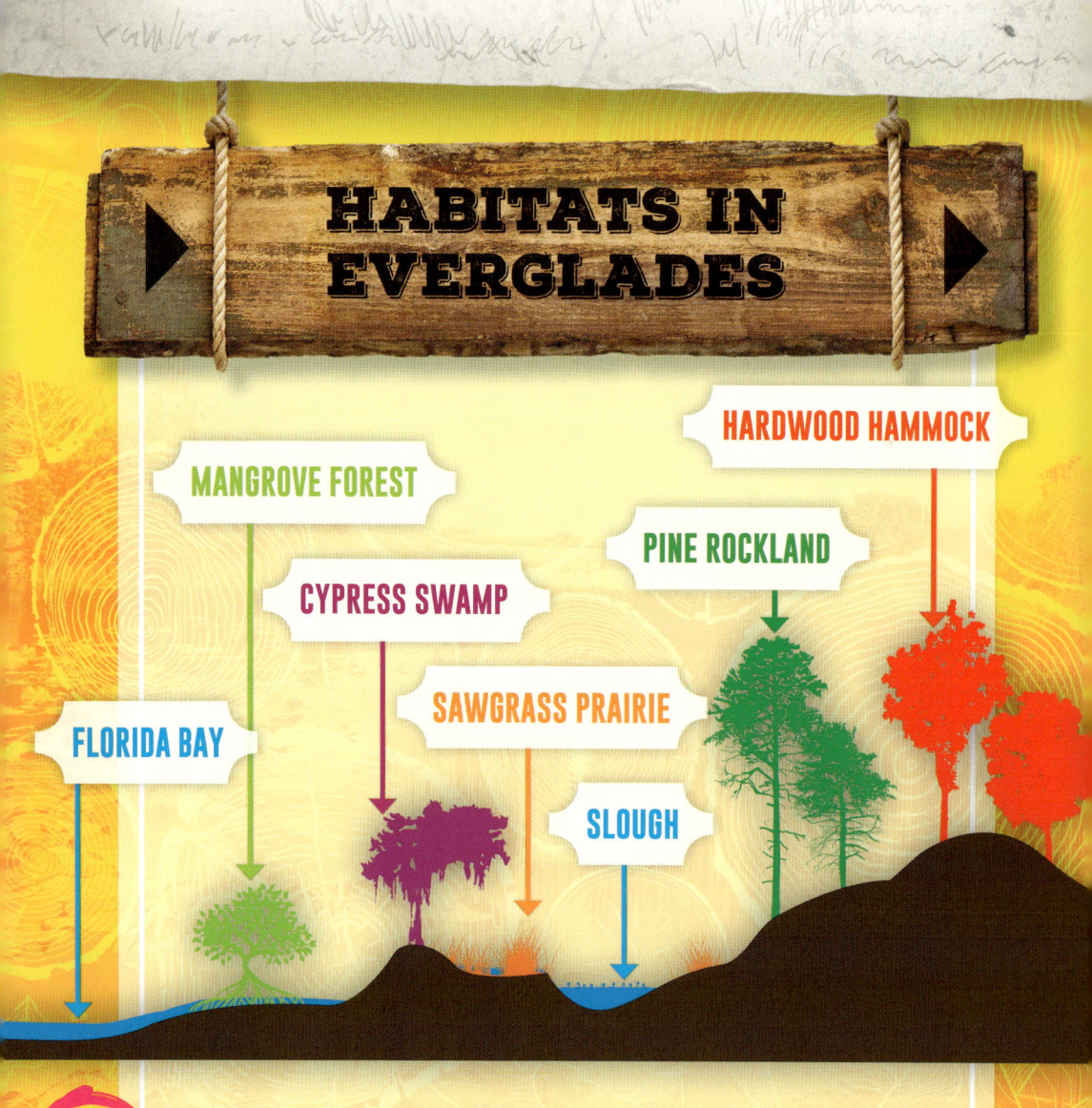

HABITATS IN EVERGLADES

HARDWOOD HAMMOCK

MANGROVE FOREST

PINE ROCKLAND

CYPRESS SWAMP

SAWGRASS PRAIRIE

FLORIDA BAY

SLOUGH

AVERAGE TEMPERATURES

JANUARY
- HIGH: 78°F (26°C)
- LOW: 54°F (12°C)

APRIL
- HIGH: 85°F (29°C)
- LOW: 61°F (16°C)

JULY
- HIGH: 91°F (33°C)
- LOW: 73°F (23°C)

OCTOBER
- HIGH: 87°F (31°C)
- LOW: 70°F (21°C)

°F = degrees Fahrenheit   °C = degrees Celsius

Everglades is the only **subtropical** national park in the United States. Temperatures are warm year-round. The dry season is from December to April. May to November is the wet season. It is **humid** with a lot of rain, thunderstorms, and occasional **hurricanes**.

PLANTS AND WILDLIFE

MARSH RABBIT

Everglades is known for its **diversity** of life! Rare Florida panthers wind through the gumbo limbo trees of the hardwood habitat. Red-bellied woodpeckers peck holes into the slash pines of the pinelands. Marsh rabbits hide between saw palmettos on the ground. Alligators rule the sawgrass prairie. They search for white-tailed deer that come out to eat sawgrass bulbs. Rare snail kites swoop down to grab snails from the grasses.

WHITE-TAILED DEER

Alligators also lurk among bald cypress trees in the cypress swamps. There, wood storks build nests on high branches. Wood ducks nibble on pickerelweed. Cottonmouths swim through the murky water.

SNAIL KITE

WOOD STORK

COTTONMOUTH

AMERICAN ALLIGATOR

Life Span: up to 50 years
Status: least concern

American alligator range = ▮

LEAST CONCERN	NEAR THREATENED	VULNERABLE	ENDANGERED	CRITICALLY ENDANGERED	EXTINCT IN THE WILD	EXTINCT

REPTILE REUNION

Everglades is the only place in the world that is home to both alligators and crocodiles.

MANGROVE FOREST

Many animal species live in the mangrove forests along the coast. Mangrove roots provide meals for sea turtles and give young sawfish a safe place to grow. Tree frogs, anole lizards, and some crabs rest up in the trees.

GREEN ANOLE

Crocodiles lurk in the shallow waters of Florida Bay. Spoonbills wade in the water, snatching up shrimp. Egrets search for gobies to eat. Manatees slowly swim in mangrove-lined waterways. They munch on turtle grass and manatee grass. Jellyfish drift through the bay's warm waters. Ospreys and eagles soar overhead, looking for prey.

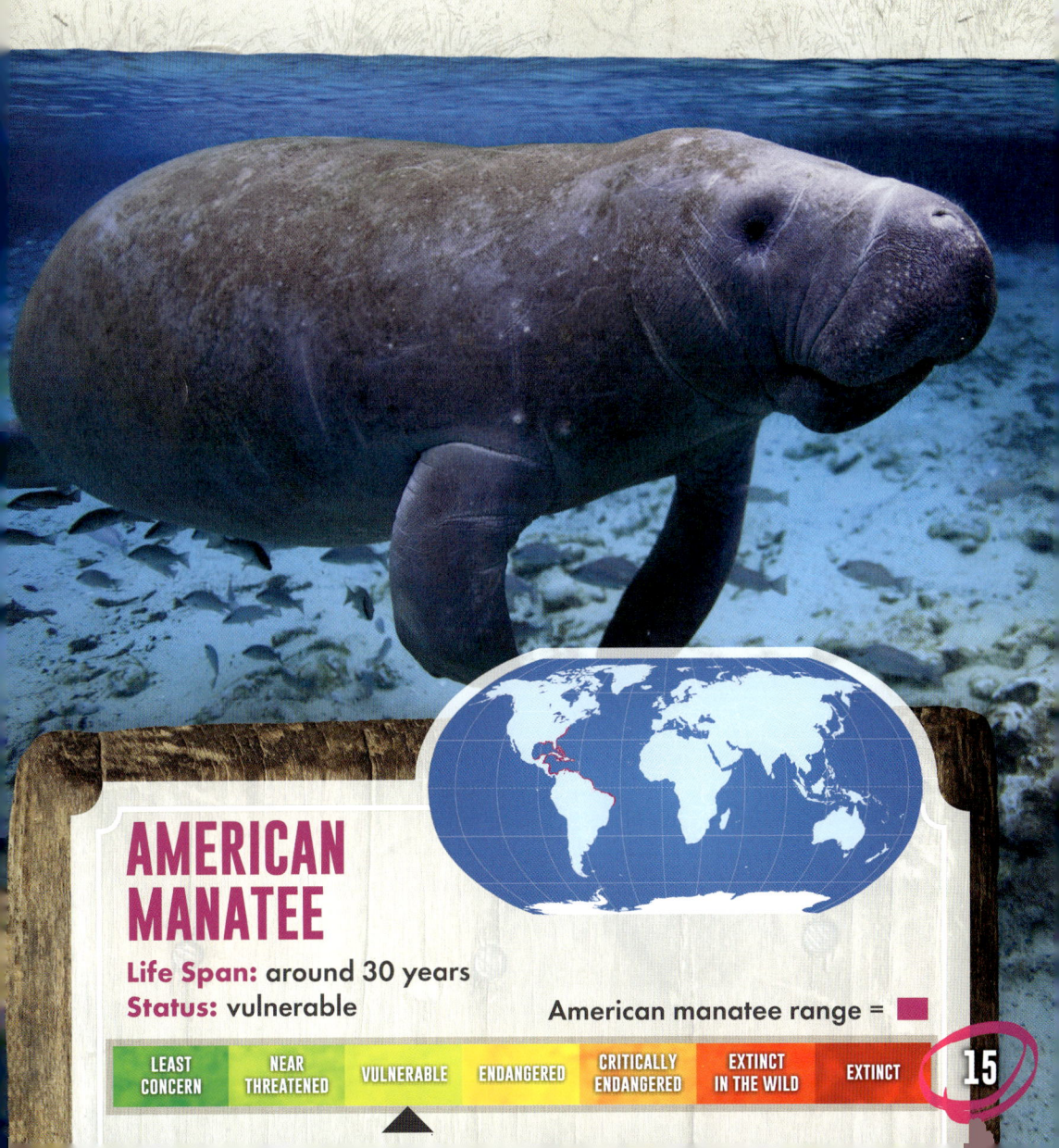

AMERICAN MANATEE

Life Span: around 30 years
Status: vulnerable

American manatee range = ⬛

LEAST CONCERN	NEAR THREATENED	VULNERABLE	ENDANGERED	CRITICALLY ENDANGERED	EXTINCT IN THE WILD	EXTINCT

HUMANS IN EVERGLADES NATIONAL PARK

The first humans arrived in what is now southwestern Florida before the wetlands even existed! This was around 10,000 BCE. Around the 1500s CE, people in southern Florida divided into tribes. The Calusa lived along the southwestern coast. They were the most powerful. They used the sea for fishing and built structures with shell tools. The Tequesta, Jeaga, and Ais peoples lived along the southeastern coast.

The Spanish arrived in southern Florida in 1513. Over the years, most of the Native Americans in the area disappeared due to deadly diseases and battles with the Spanish.

In the late 1700s and early 1800s, the Everglades wetland became home to some Muscogee people from Georgia and Alabama. They had fled from **forced relocation**. They became known as the Seminoles. The U.S. government's efforts to force them out of the area led to three Seminole Wars. Many Seminoles died or were driven out. But some hid deep in the Everglades.

People tried to drain the Everglades in the late 1800s. They thought the land was a useless swamp. By 1910, people turned much of the Everglades into farmland. More of the land was drained as more people arrived.

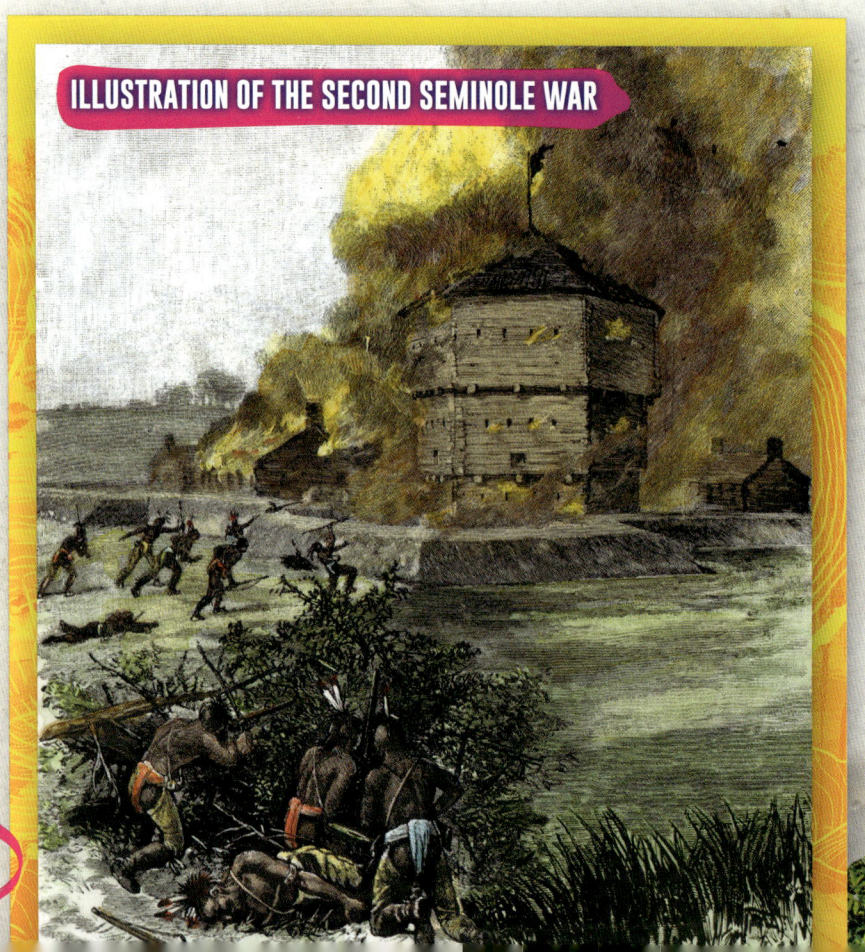

ILLUSTRATION OF THE SECOND SEMINOLE WAR

CHICKEES

Early Seminoles lived in homes called chickees. The homes stood above the wetland on cypress log stilts. Their roofs were made of palm leaves.

19

MARJORY STONEMAN DOUGLAS

Ernest F. Coe
Visitor Center

Everglades
National Park

National Park Service
U.S. Department of the Interior

Several people recognized the importance of the Everglades. In 1928, Ernest F. Coe proposed a national park in the Everglades. In 1934, the park was approved. But it took many years to buy the land. The park finally opened in 1947. However, development of the area continued. People fought back. In 1969, Marjory Stoneman Douglas created Friends of the Everglades. This group still works to protect the Everglades.

Today, more than 1 million people visit the park each year. Many Seminole and Miccosukee people live nearby on **reservations**. Some teach the history of the area or offer tours.

VISITING EVERGLADES NATIONAL PARK

There is plenty to do in Everglades! Many people explore in canoes or kayaks. They may cast lines to catch fish. Other people glide through the marshes on airboat tours. Campers boat up to chickees to spend the night.

AIRBOAT TOUR

KAYAKING

A HISTORIC SITE

Everglades is home to a Cold War missile base. Visitors can tour the base in winter.

TOP SITES

ANHINGA TRAIL

MICCOSUKEE INDIAN VILLAGE

TEN THOUSAND ISLANDS

SHARK VALLEY OBSERVATION TOWER

Some visitors stay on land. They bike along the park's paths or hike on its boardwalks. They keep an eye out for wildlife. Bird-watchers look out for rare species. History lovers can learn about the area's past at the Museum of the Everglades.

PROTECTING THE PARK

Everglades is often called the most threatened national park in the U.S. One main reason is from humans developing the land nearby. Humans drained water from the Everglades for farmland. They made changes to the land to control flooding. This harmed the **ecosystem**. Today, pollution from nearby farms drains into the area.

Climate change is another major threat. As global temperatures rise, ice caps melt and raise the sea level. The park's elevation is so low that saltwater will flood the area. This will hurt the freshwater ecosystem.

FLOODING

FARM NEAR EVERGLADES

There are many plans to protect the Everglades. In 2000, Congress passed a major law to restore the Everglades. Work for this plan will continue until at least 2035. The goal is to increase water flow and water quality in the area. The park will also introduce a new plan to Congress to bring more fresh water into the area.

INVASIVE SPECIES

Several animals and plants have been introduced to the area, including Burmese pythons and Brazilian pepper-trees. Many are harmful to the ecosystem. They eat native species and take the place of other species.

Park staff study the water to check levels and flow. They keep track of **invasive species** and remove them when they can. Other groups educate people about the Everglades. The more people who care about these wonderful wetlands, the safer they will be!

REMOVING INVASIVE SPECIES

EVERGLADES NATIONAL PARK FACTS

 **Area:** **2,188** square miles
(5,667 square kilometers)

 **Annual Visitors:**
1,155,193 visitors in 2022

 **Area Rank:** **10TH**
largest park

 **Population Rank:** **23RD**
most visited park in 2022

Date Opened:
December 6, 1947

 **Highest point:** several;
8 feet (2.4 meters)

TIMELINE

1800s
Seminole people use the Everglades as protection in three Seminole Wars

Ernest F. Coe
1866 - 1951
of Everglades National

MAY 30, 1934
President Franklin D. Roosevelt signs the law designating Everglades National Park

1928
Ernest F. Coe writes to the National Park Service and proposes a park in the Everglades

FOOD WEB

FLORIDA PANTHER

AMERICAN ALLIGATOR

WOOD DUCK

WHITE-TAILED DEER

SAWGRASS

PICKERELWEED

1969

Marjory Stoneman Douglas creates Friends of the Everglades

DECEMBER 6, 1947

Everglades National Park opens

2000

Congress passes a major law for Everglades restoration

GLOSSARY

biodiversity—the variety of life found in a certain place

climate change—a human-caused change in Earth's weather due to warming temperatures

diversity—having a variety of different things

ecosystem—a community of living things that includes plants, animals, and the environment around them

elevations—heights above sea level

estuaries—areas where the mouth of a river meets the ocean

forced relocation—the forceful removal of a people away from their homeland

gulf—part of an ocean or sea that extends into land

habitats—natural homes of plants and animals

humid—having a lot of moisture in the air

hurricanes—storms formed in the tropics that have violent winds and often have rain and lightning

ice age—a period in Earth's history when the climate was much cooler and large areas of land were covered in sheets of ice

invasive species—plants or animals that are not originally from the area; invasive species often cause harm to their new environments.

mangroves—tropical trees with tall roots that grow in shallow seawater

prairie—a large, open area of grassland

preserve—a protected area of land

reservations—lands set aside by the U.S. government for the forced removal of a Native American community from their original land

subtropical—related to parts of the world that border on the tropics; the tropics is a hot, rainy region near the equator.

wetland—an area of land that is covered in low levels of water for much of the year

TO LEARN MORE

AT THE LIBRARY

Conrad, Vicki. *A Voice for the Everglades: Marjory Stoneman Douglas*. Chicago, Ill.: Albert Whitman & Company, 2021.

Furstinger, Nancy. *Everglades*. New York, N.Y.: AV2 by Weigl, 2020.

Sexton, Colleen. *Florida*. Minneapolis, Minn.: Bellwether Media, 2022.

ON THE WEB

FACTSURFER

Factsurfer.com gives you a safe, fun way to find more information.

1. Go to www.factsurfer.com.

2. Enter "Everglades National Park" into the search box and click 🔍.

3. Select your book cover to see a list of related content.

INDEX